THE CAMBRID NOBODY KNOWS

F. A. REEVE

THE OLEANDER PRESS OF CAMBRIDGE

The Oleander Press
17 Stansgate Avenue
Cambridge CB2 2QZ

ISBN 0 900891 10 6

British Library Cataloguing in Publication Data

Reeve, Frank Albert
The Cambridge nobody knows. – (Cambridge town, gown and county ; vol. 14).
1. Cambridge – Description – Guide-books
I. Title II. Series
914.26.59.04857 DA690.C2

Photograph no. 17 is by Frith Photography. Nos. 2, 6, 7, 8, 10, 12, 13, 14, 15, and 16 are reproduced by courtesy of Christopher Hurst of Cambridge. The other illustrations are from the author's collection. The map was kindly drawn by Mrs. C. Carpenter of Haddenham.

Designed by Ron Jones

Printed and bound by Burlington Press, Foxton

CONTENTS

I. ST. ANDREW'S HUTCH

Ancient documents relating to the history of the city are now carefully preserved, but in former times many were discarded or lost, and even the valuable royal charters which are now often displayed were stowed away in drawers.

In 1928, Dr. W.M. Palmer decided to examine the ancient documents, then kept in a fire-proof room at the Guildhall, and found that they were in such disorder that he wrote a letter of protest to the mayor. A special committee was appointed, and Dr. Palmer and Mr. E.A.B. Barnard were invited to examine the documents and prepare a report. After spending two hundred hours on this very dirty task, they recommended that the documents should be cleaned, labelled, and numbered by a professional man.

In early times, the town's documents were kept in an iron box which had been presented to the Corporation by a grocer named Richard Andrew in 1459, and even after a new box had been provided, it was known as Andrew's, and sometimes St. Andrew's, Hutch. This second large chest, for a long time kept in the office of the Town Clerk, but now displayed on the landing opposite the entrances to the Council Chamber in the Guildhall, was made in 1531.

There is in existence a bill headed: "The charges payd for the new chyste provyded for the sauf kepying of the charters and other juells belonging to the town of Cambridge". The chest was made by Nicholas or Richard Otte, well-known local smiths, from oak completely covered with iron, and it weighs about a ton. The makers used 3 cwt. of iron, 11 iron plates and 1,000 nails, and it was taken to London, probably for the fitting of special locks.

Some of the city's ancient documents have been lost. In 1822 the Common Day Book for the years 1786-1792 was found to be missing, and the Deputy Clerk was blamed. A duplicate copy was made from a draft day book. Two years later, the missing book was returned by

1. *St. Andrew's Hutch*

John Inglis, a former mayor, who wrote that while putting some of his drawers to rights he had found the Common Day Book for 1786,"the loss of which had occasioned so much unpleasantness in the Corporation". As the book was a large folio volume weighing about 20 lbs., this seemed a strange explanation, especially as he himself had called a special meeting when the book was first missed.

In former times, many Corporation documents were in the private possession of Town Clerks. When Thomas Yorke died in 1756, his executor should have handed the papers to the new Town Clerk, but he placed many of them, including the treasurer's accounts for the sixteenth and seventeenth centuries, in a chest in St. Michael's Church. When the executor died, no-one seemed interested in these priceless documents, and the parish clerk was authorised to sell them.

John Bowtell, a bookbinder who lived in Trinity Street, learned that they were to be sold as waste paper, and bought them. When the next Town Clerk died, his executor gave some more treasurer's accounts to Bowtell. He now had an almost complete set for the years from 1511 to 1700, and although he believed at the time that what he had acquired were duplicate copies, made by Town Clerks for their own use, they were in fact the original documents.

Bowtell was born in 1753 and established his business in about

1780. By 1785 he was doing bindings for the University and College Libraries. In 1789 he advertised that: "Gentlemen of the University are hereby informed that they may have manuscripts or printed books transcribed, corrected, in a neat manner and on moderate terms, by applying to Mr. Bowtell, bookseller, at whose shop a specimen of the writing may be seen". The business prospered, and by 1794 Bowtell was recognised as the best craftsman for bindings in Cambridge. During the threat of a Napoleonic invasion it was difficult to obtain "Lisbons", a leather for binding exported from Spain, and Bowtell advertised that he had discovered a substitute for "paper-making in imitation of leather".

For eighteen years, Bowtell worked on the documents he had secured in order to compile a history of the town, but when no publisher would agree to terms, he bequeathed his manuscripts to Downing College. He left £3,000 to his niece and housekeeper, large legacies to other relatives, and funds for placing workhouse boys as apprentices. Above all, he left the then considerable sum of £7,000 to enlarge Addenbrooke's Hospital, and a ward was named after him.

§ *Cambridge Borough Documents,* Vol. 1, edited by W.M. Palmer, 1931.

II. THE CONDUIT OF THE FRANCISCANS

Unnoticed by most people who enter Trinity College by the Great Gate is a tap at the base of one of the towers. A notice now states that the water is unfit for drinking, but for centuries it was an important source for the townsfolk.

In 1325, the Franciscan Friars, whose house was on the site now occupied by Sidney Sussex College, acquired from seventeen different owners a strip of land one mile in length and two feet wide, from Bradrusshe, in what is now Conduit Head Road, off Madingley Road, to their Friary. In this strip they laid leaden pipes which crossed streets, brooks and the river, and passed through what is now Trinity College.

For the use of the townsfolk they provided a well-house and a pump fixed to the outer wall of the Friary, and Sidney Street was for a long time called Conduit Street, even many years after the Friary had been dissolved.

In 1439, the college of King's Hall, which later became part of Trinity, obtained the right to tap the conduit as it passed through their site, and after the Franciscan Friary was dissolved in 1538, Henry VIII granted the full rights of the conduit to Trinity College. Some time later, the portion between the college and the Friary site was discontinued.

The water from this conduit, first brought into the town about 650 years ago, still feeds the fountain in the Great Court, though it is now supplemented by an artesian well. The college has peculiar rights enabling it to prevent owners of the land through which the conduit passes from building over it in a manner which would prevent access to it throughout its course.

The Conduit Head lies about three hundred yards west of the Observatory, and an eighteenth-century building encloses the spring. The pipe goes under Madingley Road, through fields, gardens, St.

2. *The Public Water Supply at Trinity Great Gate*

John's Wilderness, and crosses the river opposite the north end of Trinity College Library, then under the hall to the fountain and the Great Gate. At various points, small stones indicate its presence below.

Carter, writing in 1753, said that the water was excellent for tea and that a great part of the townspeople used it for that purpose. Samuel Pepys, on a hot summer day in 1653, walked to Aristotle's Well (probably another name for the Conduit Head), and slaked his thirst with great draughts of cold water from the conduit.

In 1350 the Carmelite Friars were also granted a well of water somewhere in the western fields outside the town, and the mayor and commonalty agreed that they might enclose a piece of land ten feet square with a wall, and make an underground aqueduct from this well to their buildings in Milne Street (now Queens' Lane).

When, in Victorian times, it was still considered that it was not necessary to provide baths for undergraduates because terms lasted for only eight weeks, a student of Trinity acquired a tin bath and asked the bedmakers to fill it with water from the fountain. These venerable ladies were indignant, but the situation was resolved by the formation of the Waterworks Company in 1853.

Professor Sir Charles Inglis has said that the company "was really founded by two masters of colleges . . . It was not their intention really to help the inhabitants of Cambridge to have a good water supply, but a certain amount of money had been given to King's to have a fountain and Provost Okes was rather doubtful about it because there was no water; and he and Dr. Whewell put their heads together and said "Let's build a water company! And that's how we got our company".

§ Lloyd, A.H. *Ancient plumbery in Cambridge. The Cambridge Chronicle,* 15 February 1933.

III. KING CHARLES I's PORTRAIT

In St. Michael's Church there is a life-sized portrait of King Charles I. He is depicted bareheaded and kneeling before an altar, attired in a blue mantle lined with ermine, and an ermine cape.

How this portrait comes to be in the church is a mystery. There is a legend that it was presented by Charles in 1660 to the mayor of Cambridge at the time, who lived in St. Michael's parish. There is no documentary evidence of this, and no mention of the portrait in either Cooper's *Annals* or in the *Diary* of Alderman Samuel Newton who was then alive and who meticulously recorded municipal events.

The picture is first mentioned by the antiquary Cole (1714-82), who says that in St. Michael's Church is "a full length picture of King Charles the 1st in a handsome gilt frame . . . Under the said picture, in a small frame, is wrote in gold letters 'Lord, remember David, and all his troubles', Ps. 132, ver. 1". In the *Gentleman's Magazine* of May 1814, a description of the church attributed to John Bowtell mentions that "West of the pulpit is a painting of the Royal Martyr, King Charles I". A disastrous fire in 1849 destroyed a large part of the roof of the church. The painting was probably damaged, as pieces of the canvas appear to have been cut off at the sides, and for the next thirty years it was stored away in the vestry.

In 1881, the Town Council had some portraits of famous local people cleaned, and their massive frames regilded, in order to hang them in the large assembly room of the Guildhall. They wished to secure the royal portrait in St. Michael's Church, and asked the parish to surrender it. The churchwardens refused to give it up, but negotiations continued, and the minutes of a meeting of the Corporation held on 12 May, 1881, record that: "The Guildhall Committee have to report that they have been informed that Charles II on his restoration caused 100 pictures of Charles I to be painted by some pupils of Vandyck and presented the same to the Authorities of various places, and it is supposed that in Cambridge the same was sent to the Mayor and there then being no Town Hall, and the Mayor residing in the parish of Saint Michael, caused it to be placed in the Church there. The Committee applied to the Authorities of the said Parish for the pictures and received a resolution of the Vestry of which the following is a copy".

This resolution intimated that: "The Vestry is willing to entertain an application from the Corporation for the loan of the picture", and the churchwardens called a meeting of the parishioners to consider the matter. At this meeting, an amendment that the parish should refuse to lend the picture was carried.

The parishioners, now realising that they possessed an important historical portrait, decided to have it thoroughly restored, and it still hangs in the now redundant church. Whether it was originally given to the parish or to the town remains an unsolved question.

§ . Gray, A.B. *The Portrait of King Charles I in St. Michael's Church, Cambridge. Cambridge Public Library Record*, September 1935.

IV. THE TALE OF THE YALE

The animals supporting the coats of arms on the gateways of Christ's and St. John's Colleges puzzle many people, because they resemble antelopes, yet have faces more like goats, with a short beard, short ears and a low mane. The horns are not very long, but longer than the head, and the sculptors appear to have been ignorant of the laws of perspective, because one horn stretches forward over the face, while the other stretches backward over the body.

The animals are, in fact, yales, mythological beasts mentioned from very early times. They were described and illustrated in many medieval bestiaries, which were replaced later by more learned works which though still unscientific, were less fantastic than the creations of the medieval writers and artists. One horn pointing forwards and the other backwards is one of the special features of the yale.

The Rev. Edward Topsell, who resided at Christ's College in 1587 wrote a *Historie of Foure-footed Beastes* (1607) and thus described them: "There is bred in Ethiopia a certain strange Beast about the bignesse of a Sea-horse (not a 'river-horse'), being of colour blacke or brownish; it hath the cheeks of a Boare, the tayle of an Elephant, and hornes aboue a Cubit long, which are mooueable upon his head at his own pleasure like eares; now standing one way, and anone mouing another way, as he needeth in fighting with other Beastes, for they stand not stiffe but bend flexibly, and when he fighteth, he alway stretcheth out the one, and holdeth in the other, for purpose as it may seeme, that if one of them may be blunted and broken, then hee may defend himselfe with the other. It may well be compared to a Seahorse, for aboue all other places it loueth best the Waters".

It may be thought that the strange alignment of the horns originated in the imagination of ancient writers, and had no basis in fact, but some modern travellers have seen animals with horns like those of the yale.

In parts of Ethiopia, from very ancient until modern times, the

3. *Yales at the Lodge, Christ's College*

horns of some animals were mutilated and induced to change direction. The Dinka tribe to the south of the White Nile artificially trained the horns of the leaders of herds of domestic cattle so that one points forward and the other backward. In Wood's *Natural History of Man* (1868) there is a description of how Kaffirs of South Africa caused the horns of oxen to project forward and backward, or one to point upward and the other to the ground. They could be trained so that the tips met above the head, or to coalesce and shoot upwards like the horn of the fabled unicorn.

Wood wrote that the Kaffirs, skilful in their art, could never be content to leave the horns as they were. He says that Le Vaillant, during his travels in 1780-1785, came across oxen with a multiplicity of horns and many different twistings, and that the Kaffirs showed him how these results were achieved by making small incisions in the horns from the time that they began to appear.

Yales are said to have the tail of an elephant, but the animals depicted at Christ's College on the gateway and over the door of the Master's Lodge have long tails ending in three striking tufts.

§ Shipley, Arthur Everett. *Cambridge Cameos,* London 1924, pp. 64-88.

V. FROM ROMAN BATH TO BRITISH RESTAURANT

The premises of the Pitt Club in Jesus Lane were built by the Roman Bath Co. and opened in February 1863, on the site of the former coach-yard of the Hoop Hotel. The principal promoter of the venture was Henry Staples Foster, who was mayor in 1847. The elaborate entrance still remains. The bath was 56 feet by 22 feet, shelving from 4 feet 2 inches to 6 feet 2 inches, and was heated to 62°. It took seven hours to fill it with 38,000 gallons of water, and was open from May to September from 6 a.m. until 9 p.m., and from October to April from 7 a.m. until 8 p.m. On Sundays it opened only from 7 a.m. until 9 a.m.

In April it was announced that invalids could use the hot-air baths at half-price, and that free baths were available to all members of the County and Town Police Force. Why the latter should have been so favoured remains obscure. In May, receipts were said to be increasing, and a female attendant was engaged so that ladies might use the bath between 11 a.m. and 5 p.m. on Tuesdays only. In June it was said that the bath would open for working men, who were to use their own towels, from 4 p.m. until 9 p.m. on Saturdays and on Sunday mornings from 6 a.m. until 9 a.m.

The venture proved to be unprofitable owing to the lack of support, and in December the directors decided to let the premises. At this time, the Pitt Club occupied rooms above a furniture shop at 74 Bridge Street, but was given notice to quit by the end of 1865 because the building was to be demolished to make way for the eastern half of Whewell's Court. The club then moved to Jesus Lane.

It had been founded in 1835 to honour the name of William Pitt, and to assist the election of Tory members to parliament and to the local council. In 1843 it was alleged that voters had been bribed and the president of the club was summoned to appear before a committee of the House of Commons. There was more trouble when a Tory candidate for Cambridge was invited to dine with members of the club.

4. *The Pitt Club in Jesus Lane*

Whewell of Trinity, then Vice-Chancellor, wrote to the candidate begging to be allowed to state that he considered the attendance of persons *in statu pupillari* at such a dinner "highly objectionable and I hope you will do me the favour to give no encouragement to such an intention".

The political activities of the club gradually diminished, and it became purely social. In the early days the club had a distinctly aristocratic air, and many who aspired to join were turned down. Fifty years ago members dined luxuriously in a large room dominated by an oil painting of the Right Honourable William Pitt. The waiters' club livery was said to have been modelled on the dress worn in Pitt's household. In 1844 the Pitt Club committee resolved "that letters put into the Pitt letter-box be paid for from the Club money". It is believed that no other club gave a similar privilege to its members, and the custom was continued until comparatively recent times.

In 1941 the delicious food and expensive wines of former days gave way to more frugal fare when the premises became a British Restaurant.

§ Whiteley, D. Pepys. *The University Pitt Club. The Cambridge Review,* 13 and 20 November, 1965.

VI. THE MYSTERIOUS SIGN ON FITZWILLIAM HOUSE

I expect that few people, looking at the plate, p.18, will realise that it shows a part of Fitzwilliam House, the dignified gray and red brick building of 1727 facing the Fitzwilliam Museum. For many years it was the headquarters of undergraduates who were unattached to a college. The photograph was taken before 1891-2, when the shop of W. Dodd, Cabinet Maker and Upholsterer, was on the ground floor.

When this use was discontinued, and the front reinstated, a terra-cotta keyblock, seen in the photograph above the two doors on the right, was reset in its original position, and may now be seen above a window. This keyblock has in relief the date 1727, the letters I H, a cross and a Catherine wheel. For a long time, antiquarians were unable to elucidate the meaning of these figures, letters and symbols, and at one time it was thought that the cross and the Catherine wheel might have some connection with Dr. Thomas Cross, who was master of St. Catharine's College from 1719 to 1736.

St. Catherine, born in Alexandria, was sentenced by the Emperor Maxentius to be put to death on a wheel armed with knives, saws and nails, because she had converted fifty heathen philosophers to Christianity. She was rescued from this fate, but later beheaded in A.D. 305. Miracle plays founded on her life probably led to the Catherine wheel being frequently used as an inn sign. There was an inn named The Katharine Wheel in Milne Street, which was demolished when the site for King's College was being cleared, and another beside the King's Ditch near Pembroke College.

Mr. E. Saville Peck was finally able to solve the problem of the Fitzwilliam keyblock. He discovered that the house had belonged to John Halsted, a brewer who was living in Cambridge at the time. Brewers were accustomed to mark barrels of the correct size with an X, and from the fourteenth century some breweries were named The Catherine Wheel. Mr. Peck accordingly deduced that the block was

5. *Fitzwilliam House, c. 1890*

the trade sign of John Halsted, brewer, in 1727.

There is also a connection between John Halsted and St. Andrew's Street Baptist Church. When a majority of the Baptists seceded from the Meeting House on Hog Hill, they went to the present site, then called the Stone Yard. In 1721 a stable and granary belonging to John Halsted, brewer, was converted into a Meeting House.

Across the road from Fitzwilliam House, in front of the Museum, is a charming square pond with water lilies. It looks so appropriate that one might think that it was put there to enhance the appearance of the grounds, but it was, in fact, built by the National Fire Service as a static water tank. Another similar tank, which no longer exists, was constructed in front of King's College Chapel in King's Parade. Most of the static water tanks were utilitarian circular structures placed above-ground, but those in front of two of Cambridge's most famous buildings were partly sunk into the ground for aesthetic reasons.

One early morning in September 1942, people walking along King's Parade were astonished to see four canoes and a punt floating in the tank. Affixed to the side was a notice: "See the Backs and the college grounds from the river. Attendants if required". Both the Boats and the notice had been removed from the boatyard in Granta Place, nearly half a mile away.

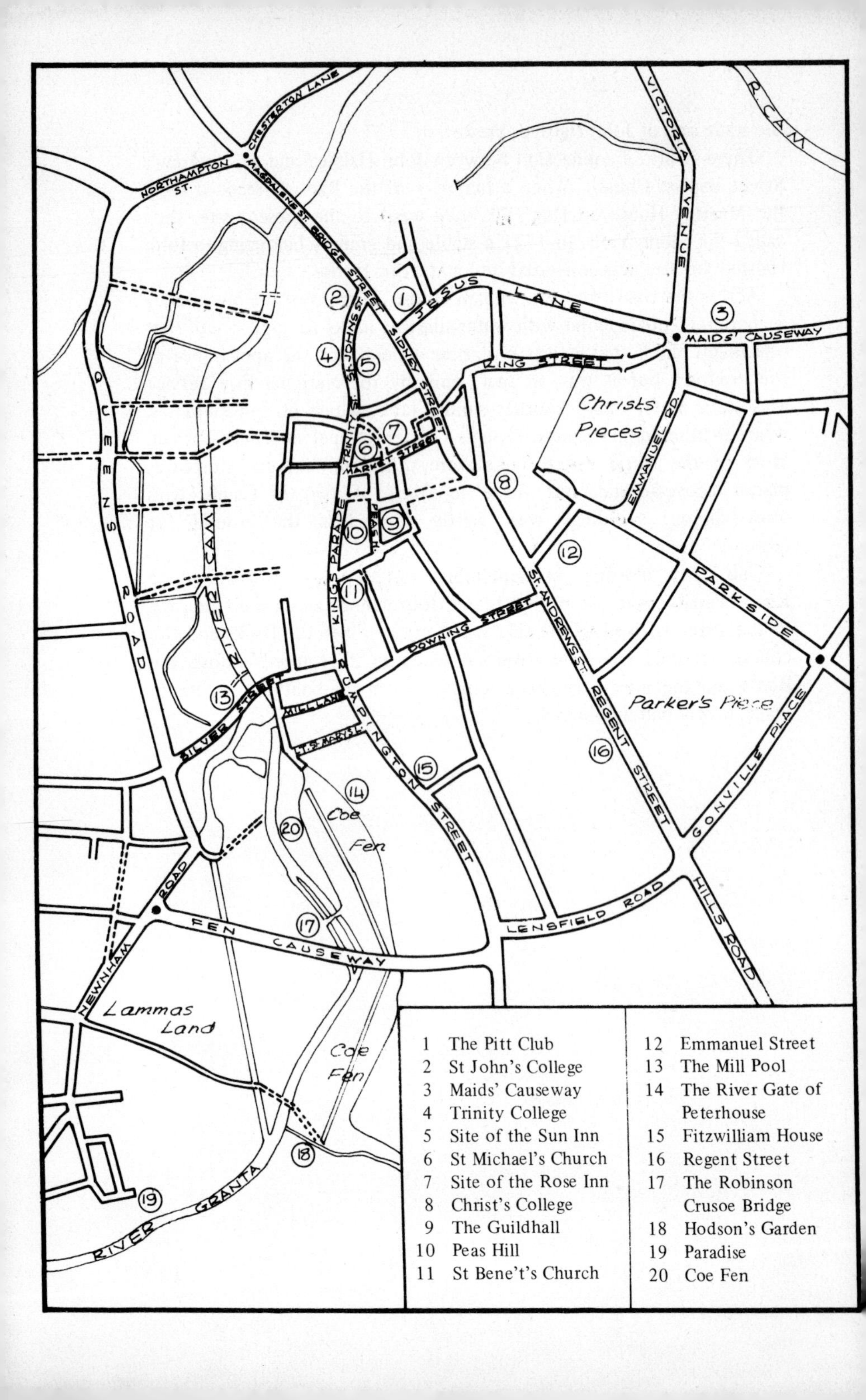
CHESTERTON LANE
NORTHAMPTON ST.
MAGDALENE ST.
BRIDGE STREET
VICTORIA AVENUE
R. CAM
JESUS LANE
MAIDS' CAUSEWAY
KING STREET
SIDNEY STREET
ST. JOHNS ST.
TRINITY ST.
Christs Pieces
EMMANUEL RD.
MARKET STREET
PEAS H.
KINGS PARADE
QUEENS ROAD
RIVER CAM
PARKSIDE
ST. ANDREWS ST.
DOWNING STREET
TRUMPINGTON STREET
SILVER STREET
MILL LANE
ST. MARYS L.
Parker's Piece
REGENT STREET
GONVILLE PLACE
Coe Fen
ROAD
FEN CAUSEWAY
LENSFIELD ROAD
HILLS ROAD
NEWNHAM
Lammas Land
RIVER GRANTA
1 The Pitt Club
2 St John's College
3 Maids' Causeway
4 Trinity College
5 Site of the Sun Inn
6 St Michael's Church
7 Site of the Rose Inn
8 Christ's College
9 The Guildhall
10 Peas Hill
11 St Bene't's Church
12 Emmanuel Street
13 The Mill Pool
14 The River Gate of Peterhouse
15 Fitzwilliam House
16 Regent Street
17 The Robinson Crusoe Bridge
18 Hodson's Garden
19 Paradise
20 Coe Fen

VII. WHERE WERE ADKIN'S COLLEGE AND WOLF'S COLLEGE?

Thomas Adkin, the only son of a rich Norfolk gentleman, took his B.A. degree in 1782 and hired a handsome suite of rooms at the White Bear Inn. This stood almost opposite the entrance to Trinity College, and had a yard extending to Sidney Street. The site later formed part of Matthew's grocery business, now Heffer's bookshop, and the entrance to the inn yard still exists. Supported by Adkin and his friends, the inn prospered, and Alderman Gurford, the landlord, became one of the wealthiest citizens. Adkin entertained lavishly, and the White Bear became known as Adkin College. He eventually became financially embarrassed, but remained a leading member of society.

Rose Crescent was formerly the yard of one of the principal inns, the Rose, with buildings on both sides, facing the market. Thomas Fuller, in his list of the ancient hostels for students in 1280, cited in his *History of the University of Cambridge* . . . (1655) states that one of them called St. Paul's Inn was now Wolf's Tavern.

For many years the Rose was kept by the Wolf family, and became known as Wolf's College because so many students lived there. When Michael Wolf died in 1618, the Rose had forty-two furnished rooms apart from garrets, and his flourishing circumstances can by gauged from the fact that among other things he owned three hundred ounces of gold and silver plate. Most of the bedrooms had carpets and hangings, and all of the beds had curtains, with a settle at the foot. There were fourteen spits, three hundred and fifty pounds of pewter, and fifty metal candlesticks. One room had pictures of St. Jerome and Susannah and the Elders. The latter would no doubt have appealed to Samuel Pepys, who often stayed at the Rose. In 1661 Pepys "went to the Rose, and there with Mr. Pechell and Sauchy and others, sat and drank all night and were very merry" and in 1668 he "lay very ill, by reason of some drunken scholars making a noise all night".

The King of Denmark lodged there in 1768, and from a window

watched the fireworks provided in his honour. Louis XVIII, King of France, stayed there for two days in 1812, and appeared on the balcony to be given a royal salute by the town militia.

From the balcony still to be seen on the building to the right of the entrance to Rose Crescent, parliamentary candidates once used to address people standing below. For centuries an enormous amount of town business was settled over the wine cups at the Rose before it reached the Council Chamber.

VIII. UNDERGROUND CAMBRIDGE

Beneath Peas Hill, near St. Edward's Church, are vast cellars covering a quarter of an acre. Two of the tunnels are a hundred yards long. They were once used as wine vaults, and during the Second World War as an air-raid shelter for four hundred persons. The Town Rental Book for 1878 records that William Potts paid 1s.3d. "for a Cellar under Market-Place, in front of the Three Tuns there, as by licence from Council, 1870". The Three Tuns, one of the most celebrated inns, visited by Pepys in 1660 "where we drank pretty hard, and many healths to the king", later became the Central Hotel, and has now been rebuilt as a Hostel for King's College. This inn had cellars reaching to the rear of the houses in King's Parade.

In the 1880's, the town authorities considered schemes for drainage, and George Bullock, a local builder, proposed that sewers should be constructed at a depth of about sixty feet. "The characteristic and distinguishing features of my scheme are", he wrote, "that the intercepting sewer should be constructed in a tunnel, and shall be made in the solid gault".

He obtained leave to construct an experimental section under Maid's Causeway, between Victoria Avenue and Fair Street, but his scheme was not accepted. There is a traditional but unfounded story that there is an underground passage between the nunnery of St. Radegund, now Jesus College, and Barnwell Abbey. It would be strange if someone in the future comes across Bullock's tunnel, and not knowing its history, assumes that it is the legendary underground passage.

Before the present shops were built on both sides of Regent Street, Professor Henslow lived in a house on the Parker's Piece side, and his stables were on the opposite side, on the site of the former Downing College brewhouse. An underground passage was constructed to connect the house and the stables, and this was visible during building operations in 1897.

6. *Entrance to the Cellars Beneath Peas Hill*

7. *Subway Below Emmanuel Street*

When Emmanuel College were making plans for their North Court, there were negotiations with the Council about the possibility of closing Emmanuel Street, but fortunately a subway was built below the street.

§ Gray, A.B. *Cambridge Memories of the Eighteen-Eighties. Cambridge Public Library Record,* December 1934.

IX. ANCIENT PUMPS

Just within the churchyard of St. Bene't's, to the left of the entrance, may still be seen the parish pump. Before the establishment of the Water Company, the inhabitants obtained water from Hobson's Conduit, wells or pumps, and the latter were often placed against churchyard walls. St. Clement's, St. Botolph's, St. Giles', Holy Trinity and the Round Church all had a pump in their churchyard walls. In one of these churchyards a sexton, when opening a grave to make a second burial in it, found that it kept filling with water. When he worked the pump nearby, the water drained away. When news of this spread, some of the parishioners decided to stop using that pump for their drinking water.

There were many pumps in the colleges. Caius had three, and the college employed a pump-mender at regular wages. One of them was against the wall of the Fellows' Garden, and from it water was drawn for washing and drinking, although there was a privy on the other side of the wall. Jesus and Queens' Colleges have a Pump Court, and a pump may still be found at King's College, just inside the entrance near Clare.

The old Pump Lane near Great St. Mary's Church took its name from the pump in the middle of it, and many of the older inhabitants will remember the fine iron pump which formerly stood on Peas Hill, near the corner of Wheeler Street. When it was damaged by traffic, it was removed to the Folk Museum.

Trumpington Street, near St. Botolph's Church, was widened in 1832 by taking a strip of the churchyard, and the pump was then transferred to Botolph Lane. The following regulations were made for this pump in 1583: "Item. It is agreed upon by ye consent aforesaid that every person housholder that shall fetch or cause to be fetched hereafter any water at ye pumpe standing in ye chirchewall in ye said parish shall paie quarterly for and towards ye mayntenançe of the said pumpe 1d. which somes shall be gathered quarterlie by suche

8. *Parish Pump of St. Bene't's*

two persons of ye said parishe as the twelve headboroughs or ye more parte shal appounte.

Item. It is agreed upon that no person shall hereafter washe eny clothes at ye said pumpe or use eny other anoyance there upon payne of forfeyture of VId. for euery time wh. forfeyture of VId. shal be to the use of ye poore and gathered by the colectors".

X. CAPTAIN COOK

On the north wall of the church of St. Andrew the Great is a memorial tablet erected by Mrs. Elizabeth Cook, widow of Captain James Cook. It bears the names of her husband: "Captain James Cook of the Royal Navy, one of the most celebrated Navigators that this or former Ages can boast of", and of her six children, who all pre-deceased her. She and two of her sons were buried in the central aisle.

There were six children of the marriage; three died in infancy, and the other three within fifteen years of the death of their father. Mrs. Cook survived her husband by fifty-six years, and the last of her children by forty-one years.

On 1 October 1780, she learned that Nathaniel, then aged only sixteen, had been lost in a hurricane off the West Indies, while serving in the *Thunderer* man-of-war. In the same month she heard that her husband had been killed in the Pacific Ocean by natives on 14 February 1779.

Three years later, Hugh, who was a student at Christ's College, died of scarlet fever, aged seventeen, and he was buried in the church which antedated the present edifice. Mrs. Cook, who was then living in Clapham, came to Cambridge to attend the funeral, accompanied by her only remaining son, Commander James Cook, who was on leave from the Navy. Thirty-five days later, James died when he was drowned while attempting to board his ship off Poole during a violent gale, and he was buried in the same grave.

After a long life saddened by so many tragic bereavements, Mrs. Cook died, aged ninety-three, on 13 May 1835, and was buried beside her two sons. On the centenary of her death, a special service was held in the church, and Sir William Birdwood, then Master of Peterhouse, who had commanded the Australian troops in Egypt and Gallipoli during the Great War, placed a wreath beside the tablet. Other wreaths were sent by the Government and the people of Australia and of New Zealand.

In her will, Mrs. Cook left £1,000 so that the memorial tablet to her husband and sons, and the inscription on the tombs of herself and her sons, might be kept clean and undefaced.

§ Stokes, *Rev. Canon Captain Cook, the Circumnavigator, and Cambridge. Cambridge Public Library Record,* June 1930.

9. *The Cook Memorial in Great St. Andrew's Church*

XI. GRAFTON GAVE US GAS

Older residents will remember the days when lamplighters came round the streets at dusk with their long poles to light the gas lamps. Many of the old lamp-posts still exist, though almost all have been converted to use electricity. One of the oldest gas lamps still lighted is affixed to the wall of No. 1 Little St. Mary's Lane.

Grafton House, which stands in Maid's Causeway, belonged to John Grafton, one of the pioneers of the gas industry, who came to Cambridge in about 1820. On 23 August, 1822, the *Cambridge Chronicle* reported that: "The building for making oil-gas for lighting the town is now being erected in Barnwell gravel-pits, and on Monday workmen started laying down pipes near Addenbrooke's Hospital". The paper added that the number of patients then in the hospital was 47.

Grafton later began to make coal gas in retorts in Gas Lane, near St. Matthew's Street, and contracted with the Improvement Commissioners, who then performed some of the duties carried out by the City Council today, to light the streets "with inflammable gas obtained from coal". He transferred his plant to River Lane, where coal arriving in lighters from King's Lynn could be unloaded.A prospectus issued by Grafton in 1826 set out a scale of annual charges for six days a week from dusk until either nine, ten or eleven o'clock. For all lights used on Sundays an additional one-sixth was charged. There were different charges for the two summer and two winter quarters, and for large or small burners.

He quoted a testimonial from gentlemen of Stamford who had lighted their premises with his gas: "We, the undersigned, have introduced into our Houses, Offices, and other premises, as might be, the Coal Gas as manufactured by Mr. Grafton, at the public works of this place; and can conscientiously declare that it is very pure, sweet and brilliant; that it is utterly divested of smoke or unpleasant smell, or effluvia; and has proved, after twelve months use, in the Drawing-

10. *One of the few remaining gas lamps, No. 1 Little St. Mary's Lane*

Rooms and best apartments, to be not in the least degree injurious to furniture; moreover, that if used with due care and economy, the consumption of it is by no means extravagant".

In 1834, an Act "to incorporate a company for better supplying with gas the town of Cambridge" was passed, and Grafton's plant and contracts were taken over by the Cambridge Gas-Light Company. A Bill of 1867 gave the company additional powers, and the name was changed to The Cambridge University and Town Gas Light Company. In the same year the Improvement Commissioners advertised for tenders for lighting the streets and for supplying private consumers, because the existing contract was shortly to expire. The tender submitted by the Gas Company was considered to be too high, and a number of local men formed another company, The Cambridge Consumers' Gas Co. Ltd. Their lower quotation was accepted.

The new company began to build a gas works on Coldham's Common, and pipes were ordered from Sheffield, but they were not able to begin to light the streets by 1 June, as they had contracted. They asked for an extension of a month, and in the meantime erected paraffin lamps on posts. These gave only a feeble light, vandals smashed some of them, and the Improvement Commissioners cancelled their contract. The old company obtained an injunction to prevent the new company from laying pipes in the streets, and although an appeal to the Lord Chief Justice reversed this decision, the Improvement Commissioners had already awarded a contract to the old company. The Consumers' company abandoned the fight when their rivals agreed to pay £5,500 for their ground and works, and guaranteed that the shareholders would not lose more than 50% of their money.

On 13 January 1870, a large gasholder erected in Newmarket Road in 1867 was blown over in a gale. 300,000 cubic feet of gas escaped and became ignited. In 1876 the Town Council considered "complaints of noxious vapours from the Gas Works claimed to destroy vegetation in the neighbourhood". The Gas Company replied that "if it is imagined the production of gas can be conducted to yield nothing but pleasant odours, then the complainants are very much mistaken.And what about the brick kilns, manure works, and most offensive of all the candle works right in the middle of the Town?".

Headly's tallow chandler's business was in Hobson Street, where candles were made by dipping cotton or rush wicks repeatedly into hot fat, until the candles were of the required size. There was another tallow candle factory at Barnwell.

XII. AROUND THE MILL POOL

When the King's and Bishop's Mills still stood at the bottom of Mill Lane, and before the coming of the railways, the Mill Pool was the scene of great activity. Barges loaded with coal, corn, oil-cake and other goods were often so numerous that one could step from one to the other from the Mills to beyond Queens' College Bridge.

Granaries covered a large area between Mill Lane and Little St. Mary's Lane, and waggons often completely filled these streets. On the Newnham side of Silver Street, Patrick Beales leased ground beside the river in 1780, and the firm built a quay, granary and warehouse. They traded in coal and corn, and their carts delivered over a wide area. When Sir George Darwin purchased these properties in the 1880's, some of the granaries and stables were pulled down, but on the wall facing the street one can still see bricked-up openings into Beales' former henhouse and stables. One large granary was converted for living accommodation and named The Old Granary.

In the nineteenth century the Corporation exacted a toll of 2d. from all persons bringing loaded carts into or out of the town. In 1824 some of the inhabitants raised a fund to challenge the Corporation in the courts, and Beales and two other leading firms refused to pay the tolls. A verdict in favour of the protesters deprived the Corporation of half of its income.

The large building beside the river was Foster's granary, later Dolby's boat-building works, and from 1911 the workshop where W.T. Pye and his son W.G. began to make scientific instruments and laid the foundation of the famous Pye radio firm. The building on the opposite side of Laundress Lane was Foster's malting-house.

Hazard's granary was in Little St. Mary's Lane, and his "old yard" later became Granta Place. He had a house in Mill Lane, divided by the Ship Inn from the dwelling of C. Finch Foster. When the latter moved to Anstey Hall at Trumpington, the inn and his house were

11. *The Bishops's Mill*

used as his offices, and adjoining buildings later became Messrs. Eaden Lilley's furniture depository and stables. Hazard and Foster were often at loggerheads. Both had a riverside wharf in Laundress Lane, and Foster claimed that he owned the right of way and erected a chain across the entrance which Hazard repeatedly broke down. In 1856 the claim was decided in Foster's favour.

There were numerous public houses in the vicinity for the bargees, carters and the men working in the granaries and mills, and the employees of the various firms favoured a particular inn. The Mill public house, now so popular in summer, was formerly call The Hazard Arms.

12. *Sign at the Mill Lane end of Laundress Lane*

The boatyard at the Anchor Inn was once the only one in the district, and when it was owned by Mrs. Robson, who later married Dolby, no boats were ever let out on Sundays. The Manager of the Anchor boatyard, Mr. Prime, who lived in Mill Lane, was the first man to introduce punts in Cambridge after he had seen them being used for racing at Henley.

At the Mill Lane end of Laundress Lane, so-called because women who washed linen for the colleges hung it out to dry close by, can still be seen a notice:

No Thoroughfare for Carriages and Horses
24th March 1857

XIII. COE FEN

The wall beside Coe Fen which encloses the grounds of Peterhouse was built in 1500, and the ancient gateway is a water-gate, as a branch of the river once flowed past. The Bishop of Ely and others, when visiting the college, could arrive by boat at the river gate, and a flight of steps on the college side enabled members to watch the water rushing by in times of flood. The arms on the Fen side of the gate are those of John Hotham, Bishop of Ely 1316-37, and those inside are of John Alcock, Bishop 1486-1500.

Until comparatively modern times, Coe Fen was very marshy. During the enquiry made by the Municipal Corporations Commission in 1833 it was stated that mire came up to horses' knees, and medical men thought that unless it were drained it would be fatal to the health of the town. A public subscription raised £150 to drain it, and early in this century the level was raised by depositing road sweepings and rubbish on it. The *Cambridge Chronicle* of 24 November 1915, said that: "Coe Fen has during the past few years been altered out of recognition . . . The Fen originally had a charm of its own, and many old inhabitants deplore its being made a deposit heap". What we now know as Robinson Crusoe's Island was formerly called Swan's Nest. Richard Blades, who leased the island in 1863 and lived in the house, now demolished, near the bridge, was drowned while returning home one night.

From 1873 the first undergraduate golfers played on the part of Coe Fen facing the Botanic Garden. Balls were often hit into the road, but there was then little traffic. The students next moved to the rough ground of Coldham's Common.

Surprisingly, because the Fen has always been common land, the base of the posts of the iron railings beside Trumpington Road bear the arms of Jesus College. The explanation is that these railings formerly surrounded Christ's Pieces when it was still a rough field

13. *The Water Gate of Peterhouse*

belonging to Jesus College. The *Independent Press and Chronicle* of 11 October 1851 reported that Christ's Pieces was to be enclosed with iron railings by Jesus College. When the town acquired the freehold in 1886, drained, levelled, and laid it out as a park, it was decided to erect a higher, unclimbable fence. Four years later, the railings removed from Christ's Pieces were used to replace low wooden railings alongside Trumpington Road.

On the other side of the road, on Empty Common, in 1839, a strange vehicle which had excited the interest of Cambridge people became bogged down. Handcock's Steam Coach, built to ply between Cambridge and London in four and a half hours, arrived for the first time on 30 September. A contemporary account described it as a big lumbering carriage, with a dozen seats. In front was the steam engine where a man "who seemed to oil the works" was seated. It was propelled by various cranks and cogs attached to the wheel of the main carriage, and driven by a man perched up in the front.

One afternoon it left the road at the Stone Bridge, broke through the wooden railings, and came to rest in Empty Common, its wheels embedded in the marshy ground. The passengers descended, and blacksmiths called to the scene took several hours to get it back on to the road. On the following day it left Cambridge for the races at Newmarket, and was never heard of again.

The large house at the beginning of Chaucer Road that is visible from Coe Fen was built by Ephraim Wayman, and its completion was celebrated by a grand house-warming party attended by about two hundred leading members of the university and the town. Wayman was adjudged bankrupt in 1888 with gross liabilities of £91,684, leaving a deficiency of £54,067.

§ Gray, A.B. *Cambridge Memories of the Eighteen-Eighties. Cambridge Public Library Record,* December 1934.

XIV. HODSON'S GARDEN

The small enclosed area on Coe Fen opposite the former ladies' bathing place was originally called Bunker's Hill Island, and was surrounded by water until this piece of common land was annexed by John Hodson in 1887. He built a summerhouse displaying his coat of arms, and enclosed the ground with a brick wall between 1902 and 1906. From the summerhouse he could watch his daughter bathing and also supervise a fish hatchery that he had constructed. The Borough Council brought an action against him, but were unable to dislodge him. He lost most of his money when Whittaker Wright, the railway speculator, fled to America, and the garden was later used by Colonel Guy Dale, the brewer, and his parents, to entertain friends to tea beside the river. The summerhouse was fortified as a blockhouse for defensive purposes in 1940.

When Mr. H. Hardy became the first custodian of the Men's Bathing Place nearby, the job was considered to be only part-time, and he did tailoring work in a section of the shed which was built in 1881. He owned a famous dog which he had trained to fetch his dinner from Little St. Mary's Lane, and his newspaper from a shop.

In July 1894, the *Cambridge Chronicle* recorded that: "The ladies of Cambridge have been provided with a bathing-place - if such it may be called in its present condition. A ladder has been erected at that point of the river just above the Iron Bridge". This was opposite Hodson's Garden. And in June 1896: "The Cambridge Town Council yesterday approved of a site on Sheep's Green at the junction of the Granta and the mill stream as a bathing place for women and authorised the payment of £150 for dressing-rooms". Miss Hardy was appointed custodian at a salary of ten shillings a week.

The "Iron Bridge" was the Robinson Crusoe Bridge built in 1898-9. A ferry from Coe Fen to the Ladies' Bathing Place was provided in 1897, and was replaced by a bridge in 1910.

14. *Hodson's Summerhouse*

Men and boys bathed naked, and when the ladies were given facilities for bathing close at hand, there were many letters in the Press urging the necessity for bathing costumes or trunks for men, but these were not made compulsory until 1909.

Gwen Raverat, in *Period Piece,* describes how ladies passing the men's sheds in boats hid behind parasols so that they would not see the naked men and boys, but usually ladies were expected to join boats at a landing-stage near Hodson's Garden. It was assumed that ladies could not manage a boat by themselves, and at most of the boatyards, men could be hired to row for them.

Hardy was succeeded as a custodian of the Men's Bathing Place by Charlie Driver, an expert swimmer and diver who saved many lives and was usually known as "China" Driver because of his prowess in retrieving plates thrown into the river. He was also a gymnastics instructor, fearless wicket-keeper and a dashing outside-right.

XV. PARADISE

Today, the name Paradise designates the small island beside the nature reserve adjoining Owlstone Croft, but formerly it embraced the whole area up to the Lammas Land. There were once tennis courts known as the Paradise Courts on the University Hockey Ground.

References to Paradise go back a long way. The earliest mention of bathing in Cambridge records that in 1567 the son of Walter Haddon, while at King's College, was drowned "while washing himself in a Place in the river Cham called Paradise", and William Stukeley, the eighteenth century antiquary, when at Corpus College in 1704 wrote: "I used to frequent, among other lads, the river in Sheep's Green, and learnt to swim in Freshman's and Soph's Pools, as they are called, and sometimes in Paradise, reckoning it a Beneficial Exercise". And it was here, in 1811, that Byron's brilliant friend Matthews became entangled in weeds and was drowned.

On the thickly wooded island of Paradise, about two acres in extent, is an old house which was once a public house and a favourite resort for students. Until recent years one could see, on the side of the house facing the river, the words PARADISE HOUSE, F.R. HYDE, HOME BREWD ALES. At the far end of the island, where there is a smaller island, a cold bath was constructed for the use of the ladies of Newnham College.

The larger area now called Owlstone Croft was formerly called Paradise Garden. In 1740 it was taken over by Mr. Rowe, who had introduced into Cornwall a system of forcing early vegetables for the London market, and here he produced them in a scientific way. His son Richard became associated with a Dutch bulb grower, outstripped all competitors in the production of beautiful flowers, and invented the hyacinth glass for growing bulbs in water only. When the estate was bought in 1879 by Major R. Calvert, Chief Constable of the County Police, the grounds were described as "not to be surpassed in the

15. *Paradise House*

Neighbourhood for Growth and Beauty" and they had "upwards of 355 square yards of Brick Walls all clothed with choice Fruit Trees". The house was rebuilt, with cottages for a coachman and a gardener, in 1881. In 1914, A.B. Lassiter used it as a school for young women.

Before the locks on Sheep's Green were improved, Paradise House was often completely cut off by floods. Gunning, in his account of the great flood in 1795, says that the water in the house was seven feet deep, and that the occupants spent an anxious night, fearing that the walls might give way. Furniture washed out of the rooms was found later near Silver Street Bridge, and provisions had to be sent to the house by barge. The house was surrounded by water most recently during the Fen floods of 1947.

A music critic wrote that in Delius' opera, *A Village Romeo and Juliet,* the intermezzo, *The Walk to Paradise Garden,* portrays star-crossed lovers making their way to an old riverside inn, *The Paradise Garden,* to spend one last carefree day together.

It is curious that there was a similar pleasure garden in Oxford, as a writer at the time of Queen Anne recorded that: "We next went to Paradise-garden at the end of the town, by a tavern; there are countless little cabinets partitioned by hedges, where fellows drink in summer".

XVI. LAND OF HOPE AND GLORY

One of the highlights of the last night of the Promenade Concerts is when the vast audience in the Albert Hall join in singing *Land of Hope and Glory*. The author of the words, A.C. Benson, is buried in St. Giles' Cemetery, Huntingdon Road. Benson, who was Master of Magdalene College and the author of a number of popular books, died in 1925.

Elgar's *Pomp and Circumstance March No. 1* was first performed as an orchestral piece in Liverpool in October 1901, and in London a few days later, and was an immediate success. It was King Edward VII who suggested to Elgar that words should be written for the trio,

16. *A.C. Benson's Grave in St. Giles' Cemetery*

middle section. The composer had been invited to compose a Coronation Ode for a state performance at Covent Garden on the eve of the coronation in June 1902, and he asked Benson, then a housemaster at Eton, to write some verses. The seventh and final section of the Ode was *Land of Hope and Glory,* for solo contralto, chorus and orchestra, the tune being adapted from the march. The King's coronation had to be postponed when he had to undergo an appendix operation, and *Land of Hope and Glory* was first performed as a song by Dame Clara Butt in June 1902. The *Coronation Ode* was first performed at the Sheffield Festival in October 1902. In August 1914 Elgar thought that the words of *Land of Hope and Glory* were no longer appropriate, and he asked Benson to write new words, but the original version had by this time become so firmly established that the new words found no favour with the public.

XVII. THE HORSE GRIND FERRY AND ROEBUCK HOUSE

The bridge opposite the Green Dragon public house in Water Street, Chesterton, replaced the Horse Grind Ferry. There were two ferries, the larger for horses and carts. In Victorian times, horses towing "party boats" hired by people making an excursion on the river, or going to the May Races, took the ferry to cross to the towpath on the opposite bank.

Bates' Ferry, on the site of the Victoria Avenue Bridge, was the first to disappear. The Fort St. George Ferry, owned by W. Pauley, had been operated for fifty years before it sank, and Dant's Ferry, near the Emmanuel College boathouse, ran from 1868 until it was superseded by the footbridge in 1927.

B. Jolley, a ferryman who had a fen-pattern punt just below the Pike and Eel, was widely known as "Charon". W. Everett, who was at Trinity College in 1859, relates that on his way to the boat races he waited "till the regular boatman came back with his last load, with his clean blue boat, and his hat showing the ribbon of the head of the river. He is at once saluted as "Charon" by a dozen voices, and imploring us to "step steady, gentlemen", soon punts us over on the verge of foundering". A tombstone in Chesterton churchyard records his fame.

On 10 June 1905, the concluding day of the May Races, two undergraduates did not "step steady", but jumped aboard a heavily laden ferry at Ditton Plough, causing it to capsize. More than twenty people were thrown into the river, and although there were many boats and people close at hand, three young women were drowned. In a previous accident at the same spot, in 1883, a man was drowned when the ferry overturned.

I suppose that few of the thousands of people who cross the Green Dragon footbridge know that in the eighteenth century baptisms took place here. In 1767 they were witnessed by a crowd of about 1,500

17. *The Horse Grind Ferry, c.1910*

persons who stood on the banks or climbed trees.

A few yards away, at the corner of Water Street and Ferry Lane, stands Roebuck House, once the home of Robert Robinson, the influential Baptist minister. Born at Swaffham in Norfolk in 1735, his mother was the daughter of a propertied gentleman who had married beneath her and was soon deserted by her husband. As a hairdresser's apprentice in London, Robinson was considered to be eccentric because he read until four or five o'clock in the morning.

In 1759, when we was 23, he came to Cambridge and preached for the first time to the Baptists who met in a barn, formerly a granary, described as "a damp, dark, cold, ruinous, contemptible hovel", in the Stone Yard in St. Andrew's Street. The members of the church numbered only thirty-two, of whom nineteen resided outside Cambridge. In 1761 Robinson became the minister at a salary of £3.12s. for the first six months. He soon attracted larger congregations, and in 1764 a meeting house to seat 600 persons was built. A visitor in 1775 declared that nearly two hundred undergraduates were at one of his lectures and that they behaved well, but at other times, the students disrupted his services, and an American minister said that "Never did I see such heathenish impiety during divine service as in the Cambridge undergraduates".

In 1773 Robinson moved with his wife and eleven children to Roebuck House, and purchased it two years later. He pulled down and rebuilt part of the house, improved the garden by embanking and raising the level of a mud-shoal, and constructed a bath for baptisms. His salary was still small, but he was helped by Ann and Susannah Calwell, two rich ladies who came to reside in the house of Christopher Anstey at Trumpington in 1777.

In 1782 he bought a farm, rebuilt the house and outbuildings, and to his great delight began to live the life of a farmer. In 1782 he bought another farm and began business as a corn and coal merchant. Writing on the 26 May 1784, he described how a typical day began. He rose at 3 a.m., roused the girls for milking, went to the farm to wake up the horse-keeper and fed the horses while he got up. He told a boy to suckle the calves and clean out the cow-house, went to the paddock to look at the calves, then to the ferry to ensure that a boy had scooped and cleaned the boats.

He next returned to the farm to examine the eight ploughhorses, mended whips, pumped water, saw that the pigs were fed, and went back to the river to buy a lighter of turf and sedge for fuel. He called the men for breakfast, cut bread and cheese for the boys and filled their water-bottles, sent out ploughmen, and had his own breakfast at 5 a.m.

Before 9 a.m. he had sent two men to ditch, two to chop sods to spread on the land, two to muck out a yard, and three men and six women to weed the wheat; the carpenter was given his orders and the wheelwright told to mend carts and ladders. At 9 a.m. he had dinner, entertained some visitors, then changed his clothes to go to preach at a meeting.

Although he led such a strenuous life, he was no doubt happy: "Here I weed my garden, plough the silver stream with my two-oar boat, read, scribble, contemplate . . . if I awake in the night, the nightingale beneath my window lulls me to rest again". In 1781 the London Baptists, lamenting that they had no authentic history of the English Baptists, asked Robinson to undertake the task, and it was published in 1790. He died suddenly at Birmingham in that year, but his daughter Julia is buried at Chesterton churchyard.

§ Dyer, G. *Memoirs of the Life and Writings of Robert Robinson, late Minister of the Dissenting Congregation in St. Andrew's Parish.* Cambridge 1796.

§ Nutter, B. *The Story of the Cambridge Baptists and the Struggle for Religious Liberty* 1912.